POPULAR PIANO SOLOS
JAZZ

ARRANGED BY FRANK BOOTH

WISE PUBLICATIONS
LONDON/NEW YORK/SYDNEY

EXCLUSIVE DISTRIBUTORS:
MUSIC SALES LIMITED
8/9 FRITH STREET, LONDON, W1V 5TZ, ENGLAND
MUSIC SALES PTY. LIMITED
120 ROTHSCHILD AVENUE, ROSEBERY, NSW 2018, AUSTRALIA

THIS BOOK © COPYRIGHT 1983 BY
WISE PUBLICATIONS
UK ISBN 0-7119-0394-8
UK ORDER NO. AM 33861

DESIGNER: HOWARD BROWN
COVER PHOTOGRAPH: TONY STONE ASSOCIATES LTD.
MONTAGED BY NICK WHITAKER
COMPILATION: PETER EVANS
ARRANGER: FRANK BOOTH

MUSIC SALES COMPLETE CATALOGUE LISTS THOUSANDS OF
TITLES AND IS FREE FROM YOUR LOCAL MUSIC BOOK SHOP,
OR DIRECT FROM MUSIC SALES LIMITED. PLEASE SEND A
CHEQUE OR POSTAL ORDER FOR £1.50 FOR POSTAGE TO
MUSIC SALES LIMITED, 8/9 FRITH STREET, LONDON W1V 5TZ.

TYPESET BY CAPITAL SETTERS

PRINTED IN GREAT BRITAIN BY
REDWOOD BOOKS, TROWBRIDGE, WILTSHIRE

CONTENTS:

TAKE FIVE

MUSIC: PAUL DESMOND

To Coda ⊕

D.S. al Coda

⊕ *CODA*

TUXEDO JUNCTION

WORDS: BUDDY FEYNE
MUSIC: ERSKINE HAWKINS, WILLIAM JOHNSON AND JULIAN DASH

ROUND MIDNIGHT

WORDS & MUSIC: COOTIE WILLIAMS AND THELONIOUS MONK

DON'T GET AROUND MUCH ANYMORE

WORDS: BOB RUSSELL MUSIC: DUKE ELLINGTON

CARAVAN

DUKE ELLINGTON, IRVING MILLS AND JUAN TIZOL

I'LL REMEMBER APRIL

WORDS & MUSIC: DON RAYE, GENE DE PAUL AND PATRICIA JOHNSON

MANTECA

WORDS & MUSIC: DIZZY GILLESPIE AND GIL FULLER

IS YOU IS, OR IS YOU AIN'T
(MA' BABY)

WORDS & MUSIC: BILLY AUSTIN & LOUIS JORDAN

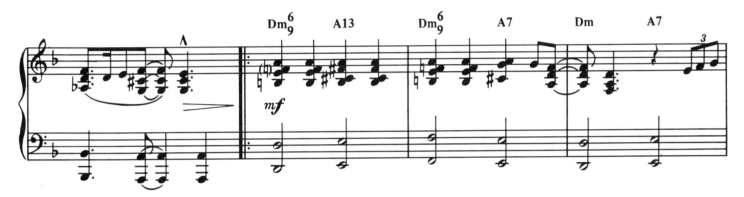

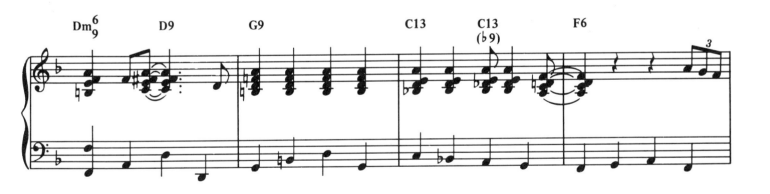

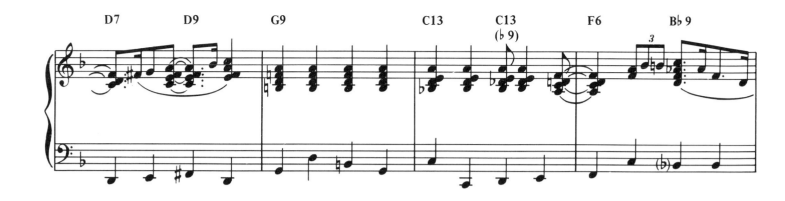

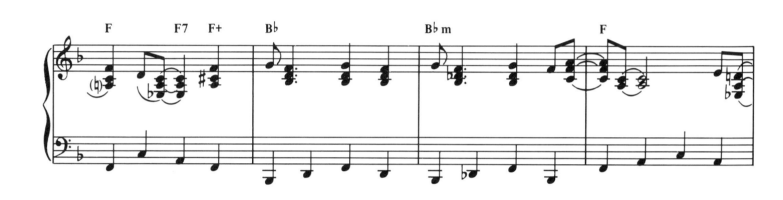

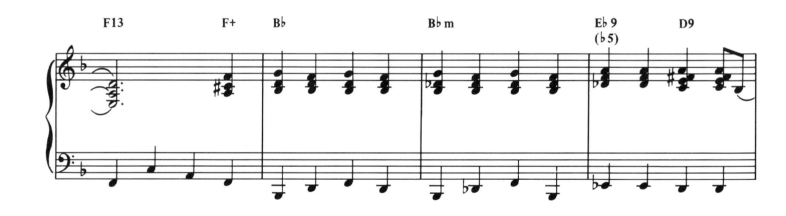

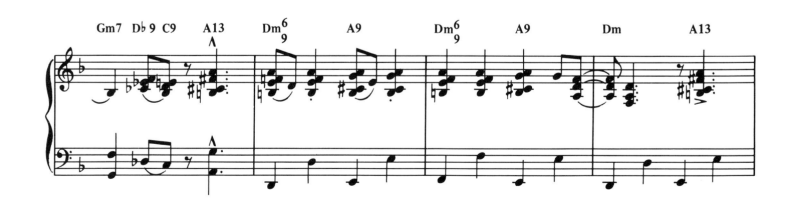

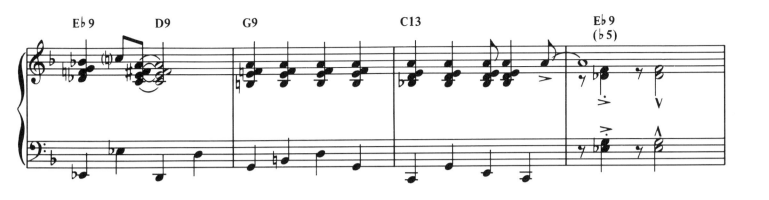

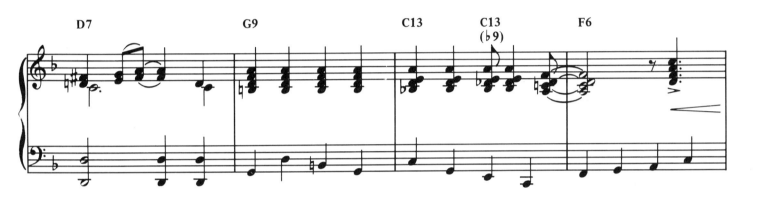

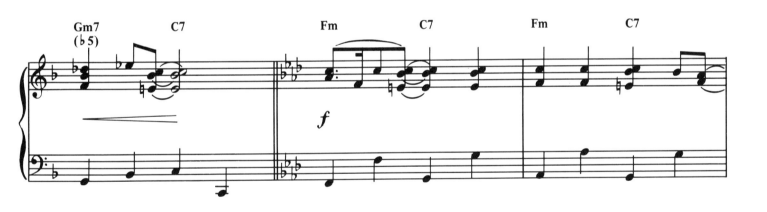

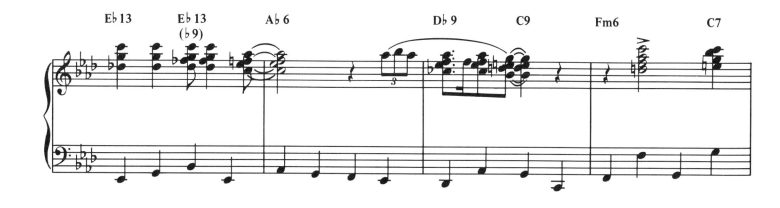

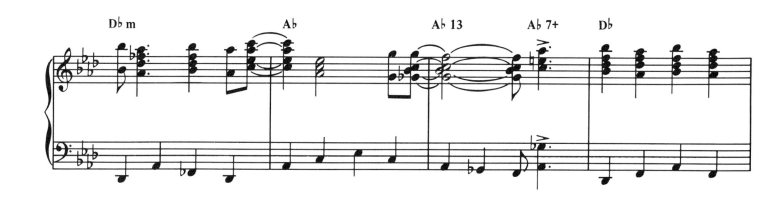

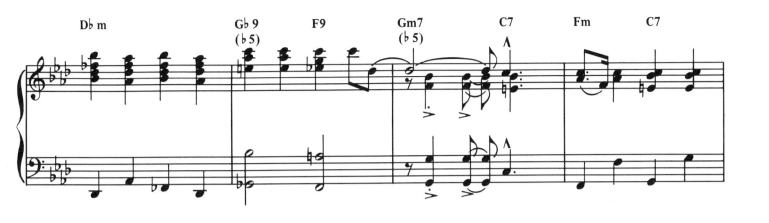

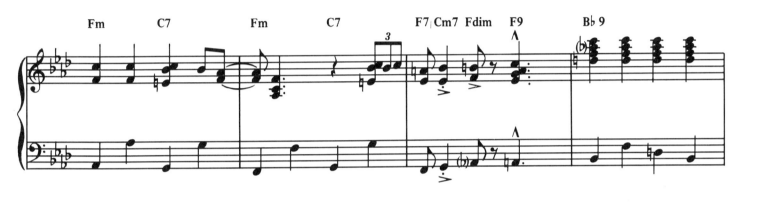

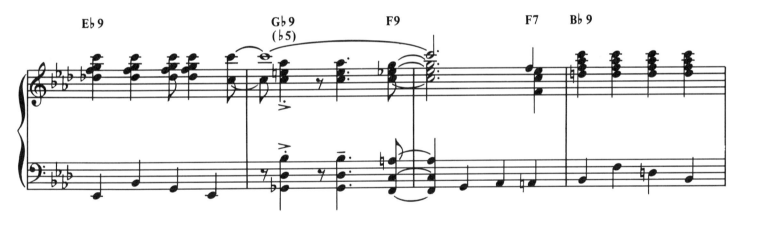

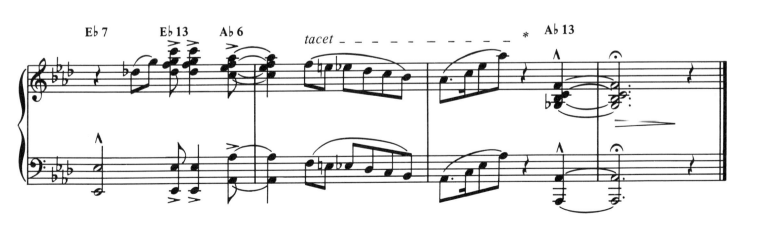

LONESOME ROAD

WORDS: GENE AUSTIN   MUSIC: NATHANIEL SHILKRET

31

BETWEEN THE DEVIL AND THE DEEP BLUE SEA

WORDS: TED KOEHLER MUSIC: HAROLD ARLEN

ON THE SUNNY SIDE OF THE STREET

WORDS: DOROTHY FIELDS MUSIC: JIMMY McHUGH

UNDECIDED

WORDS: SID ROBIN MUSIC: CHARLES SHAVERS

STRUTTIN' WITH SOME BARBECUE

WORDS: DON RAYE MUSIC: LOUIS ARMSTRONG

AFRICAN WALTZ

WORDS & MUSIC: GALT MACDERMOT

LAZY RIVER

WORDS & MUSIC: HOAGY CARMICHAEL AND SIDNEY ARODIN.

IN WALKED BUD

THELONIOUS MONK

Ab   Cbdim Eb7   A7   Ab6   To Coda ⊕

D.%. al Coda

⊕ CODA   Gb(add9)

TAKING A CHANCE ON LOVE

WORDS & MUSIC: JOHN LATOUCHE, TED FETTER AND VERNON DUKE

56

I'M GONNA SIT RIGHT DOWN
AND WRITE MYSELF A LETTER

WORDS: JOE YOUNG MUSIC: FRED E. AHLERT

Bounce tempo

FEVER

WORDS & MUSIC: JOHN DAVENPORT AND EDDIE COOLEY

Moderate jump beat

EARLY AUTUMN

WORDS: JOHNNY MERCER
MUSIC: RALPH BURNS & WOODY HERMAN

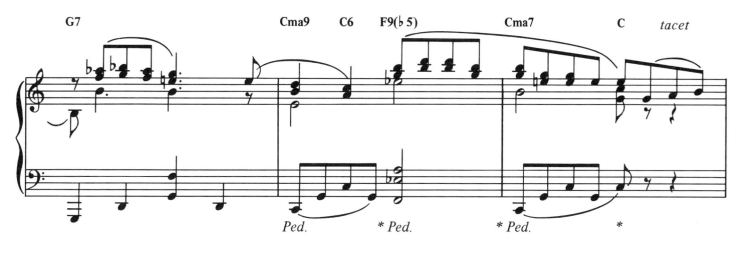

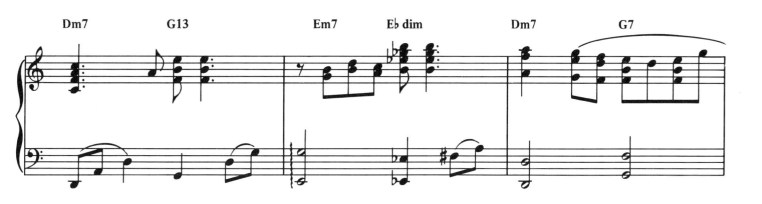

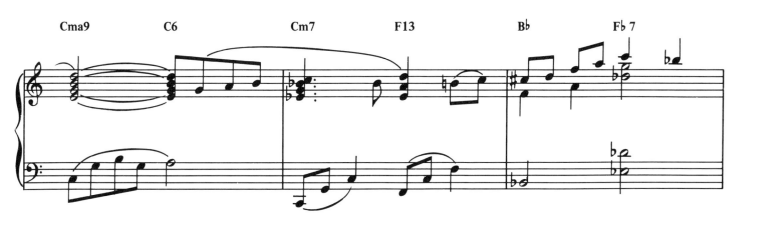

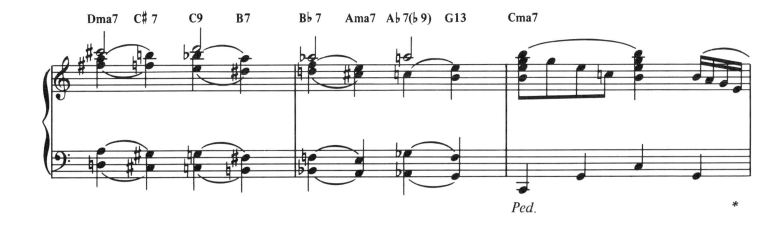

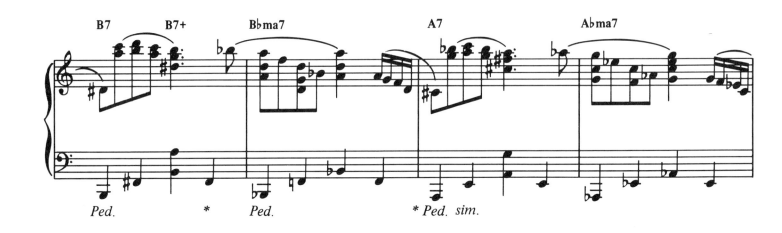

12/96(26647)